Aunt Lisa,
Thanks so much
for supporting me!
Be Blessed,
Tabitha

MW00443727

Daily Devotionals For Survivors Of Sexual Abuse

Tabitha M. Bellamy-McKinley

Table of Contents

Our Story is Centuries Old

In times of pain and questioning, I often wondered how God could allow incestuous abuse to happen to me. There are others in my own family who had also been abused by my father, yet he was still free on the streets. It seemed so puzzling to me. I just couldn't understand how a person could abuse family member after family and get off "scot free" so to speak. One day I randomly happened to come upon a story in the bible that was a little like mine. It is a story that is largely undiscovered. I know I had attended church all of my life and had never heard it mentioned. It is one of actual rape and incest in the family of David when he was king.

In 2 Samuel 13 there is a story about Amnon and how he lusted after his half-sister Tamar. He knew that he could not do anything to her because she was a virgin. Over time, he allowed his lust to consume him until he became physically sick with thoughts of her. An evil cousin convinced Amnon to tell their father David that the only thing to make him well again would be to eat bread prepared at his bedside by Tamar. David agreed, and sent Tamar in to her brother's side to prepare food for him. Once in his room, Amnon sent all servants away and tried to convince Tamar to *"Come lie with me, my sister"* 2 Samuel 13:11. She refused and asked him a very important question *"Whither shall I cause my shame to go?"* 2 Samuel 12:13. Tamar knew something that all victims of sexual abuse share-there would be shame if she was forced to sleep with a family member. Her brother Amnon did not listen to her request and the bible says that *"being stronger than she, forced her, and lay with her"* 2 Samuel 13:14.

From there the story goes on to say that immediately he hated her more than he loved her. He kicked her out of his room, and bolted the door behind her. She was violated and ashamed and tore the clothing she wore that symbolized her virginity. How horrible, to have her virginity stolen from her, not shared in a loving covenant of marriage, but stolen and by a family member no less. And then to make matters worse, he turned on her in anger as if she had done something wrong!

I have experienced this. As a pre-teen I was abused by my father, a pastor. Then, instead of loving me and protecting me, he beat me. It was like he hated me more, but at the same time lusted after me. It made me feel like I had done something wrong. I began to hate my body. I would constantly compare my body to other women around me in order to try to see if there was something different about me as a girl that made me more attractive to a man. Like Tamar, I too wanted to know where my shame would go. I tried to hide it in academic achievements, professional organizations, my sorority, community service, and living in a perfectly controlled environment where no one could enter to touch my heart.

This is a story all too familiar to many of us. We have been taken advantage of by those who were supposed to love and protect us. We have had our bodies violated by people who did not respect God's covenant between a man and woman and the sacred place for sexual intimacy within marriage. We have been left with the shame. We have torn our outward signs of our virginity and purity by giving our bodies to others in sexual promiscuity, rage, achievements, isolation, and drug or alcohol abuse.

But like Tamar, know that God has not forgotten us. He has seen the actions of those we accuse, and knows that we are innocent. He knows that we had desires to be pure, holy and acceptable; to grow in a world where we were loved and protected, happy and playful instead of suspicious and skeptical. In the end of the thirteenth chapter of second Samuel, two years after Tamar's assault, her brother Absalom kills Amnon. Now, please don't misinterpret what is going on here. I don't think this part is in the text to allude to us that our abusers will be killed. I do however, think it is here to show us that God knows and does not forget. It may seem like our abusers have gotten away with a heinous crime. After all, who can place a price on the life of an innocent person? For us, the abuse is worse than death. The victim of a murder must never face themselves in the mirror wondering what he or she did to deserve such a thing. Victims of sexual abuse are killed emotionally and mentally, and left to themselves to live inside of a corpse. There is no greater pain than to be trapped inside of a dead body.

If you can relate to any of the things you've read so far, this book is for you. If you feel alone, I encourage you to read it. If you feel like God has forgotten you, has abandoned you, or even hates you, then YOU are my target audience. This book is not written in the third person. It is not written by a person who is a self-proclaimed "expert" on abuse. I have no background in counseling. I am simply the daughter of a pastor, and the granddaughter of two. I was raised in the church all of my life with lots of anger toward God and many times questioned my faith.

People always told me to read the bible when I felt depressed or suicidal as it related to my abuse, but I had no idea where to begin. When I wrote this, I again felt like I had no idea where to start. God showed me day-by-day what to write and how to write it. He revealed new things in scripture that are unique to _our_ experiences. It may be hard to grasp the concept of a devotionals book for individuals who have been sexually abused. It took me a decade to write this. There will be a plethora of emotions that you experience as you turn each page. I encourage you to read one devotional a day, and read the scripture reference in its entirety. End each reading with a prayer of strength and courage. If you do not know any prayers, I am including one at the end of this passage. Find one friend or loved one you feel you can be vulnerable with as you begin your journey. It's time to be free. It's time to be healed. It's YOUR time!!!

Be blessed,

Tabitha

DAILY PRAYER

Father God, I know that I cannot make this journey without you. Today I ask that your joy be my strength, that your peace guard my heart and mind, and that you help me renew my mind with Your Word. Create in me a clean heart and renew a right spirit within me. I know that I can do all things through Christ who strengthens me, and with You all things are possible. I come to You with the faith of a mustard seed, and ask You to help me use it to move the mountains of doubt, fear, insecurity and depression in my life.

Lord, in all that I say and do, use me to do Your Will today.

In Jesus' name, Amen.

9-1-1

Hello?

Hello?

I'd like to report a crime

It's a robbery. It's a murder too.

Who was the victim? Me.

What was taken? Everything.

I was robbed of my purity, my cleanliness, of looking at myself without shame, or doubt, or fear, or insecurity. I was robbed of my innocence, of my safety, of my future, of my past. I was robbed of everything I was or everything I could be. My spirit was taken, my soul was snatched, my foundation was destroyed. Everything that's inside me was ransacked, torn apart, and the pieces strewn about as if they never mattered.

Of course I'm talking to you. That doesn't mean I'm really alive.

Other people see sunshine, I see a bright light that seeks to shine in a place where I won't let anyone in. People hear laughter, but I think "They're laughing at ME." When people look at me, I know they see a corpse. They wonder why I'm not as happy as they are, but they have no idea what it's like to be trapped inside a dead body. A body that's filled with vile, rotting flesh that stinks everywhere I take it. I can't wash it away. Perfume doesn't help. The stench is so engrained in my head that I cannot allow another person to get too close to me for fear that they might smell it and run away.

Yes, I'd like to report a crime.

Is there anyone there who can help me?

Day 1: A Child Sacrifice

David was a boy out watching sheep for his father. He killed a lion and a bear, both of his own choosing. He was being a kid, playing around his older brothers, and someone used him to face a giant because the adults in his life were not equipped or unafraid enough to face him themselves.

What if he had died? Would this have been such a heroic story of salvation? Was it ok to sacrifice a child to save adults from their own problems? He was a boy. When he became a man he was not able to function fully as a man because he had not resolved his boyhood feelings such as sharing, patience, and lust. The adults in his life forced him to be something he was not before his time and he ended up living a life full of repentance because of it.

Take for instance the story of Bathsheba. David saw a woman who was bathing from afar and wanted her. Because he had not been through a regular childhood and was simply elevated to a status of royalty as a boy, it seemed he had no real concept of patience and not having something that wasn't his. According to the bible in 2 Samuel 11: 2-4 *"And it came to pass in an eveningtide, that David arose from off his bed, and walked upon the roof of the king's house: and from the roof he saw a woman washing herself; and the woman was very beautiful to look upon. And David sent and inquired after the woman. And one said, Is not this Bathsheba, the daughter of Eliam, the wife of Uriah the Hittite? And David sent messengers, and took her; and she came in unto him, and he lay with her; for she was purified from her uncleanness: and she returned unto her house. And the woman conceived, and sent and told David, and said, I am with child."*

Once David discovered this, he tried to make things better by bringing her husband Uriah home from battle, hoping he would sleep with Bathsheba and the pregnancy scandal would go away. Uriah was a loyal soldier to David and did not leave the king's gate, but slept there instead of being with his wife. David knew he could not hide the pregnancy and had Uriah killed in battle then married Bathsheba. That is Old Testament "baby mama drama"!

Because of David's sin against God, the prophet Nathan announced to David that the baby conceived in sin, dishonesty and lust would die. David confessed to the prophet that he had done wrong, *"And David said unto Nathan, I have sinned against the LORD. And Nathan said unto David, The LORD also hath put away thy sin; thou shalt not die"* 2 Samuel 12: 13.

Isn't this good news for us? Perhaps we have conceived lives based in sin. Sin that stems from events that are not our fault, and like David and Bathsheba's first baby, those things must die, but we will **not die**. After the death of the baby,

David worshipped God, and he conceived a new baby with Bathsheba named Solomon.

God did not have to change the characters in order to change the outcome. If we are willing to confess that we in our own hurt have sinned against God, He will allow those things within us that are proof of our iniquity to die and give us a second chance. Today, worship God. Allow Him to cleanse you, to change you, to kill those things that are outward evidence of your inward pain, and to give you a fresh start.

Day 2: Abuse of the Powerless

Sexual abuse is about more than sex, it's about power. It's about a person who has power or control dominating a person who does not. It's about a stronger person taking advantage of a weaker one. For me, I was 12, my abuser was 41. I was a girl, he was a man. As awful as it is, God is not new to the concept of someone in a position of no power being used to fulfill the dream of a person in authority.

Take for instance the story of Hagar. Hagar was an Egyptian slave. Egypt is known as the bedrock of civilization based on its many sophisticated economic, mathematical and architectural systems. Hagar was given to a "less civilized" Hebrew tribal leader Abraham and his wife Sarah to be their servant. She was to be ruled by Sarah-the wife of Abraham and serve as her handmaiden. As is known in the bible, Abraham and Sarah were very wealthy people and had many cattle, and a great caravan of servants and other family, however they could not bear a child.

God had made a promise to Abraham that he would one day be the father of many nations, but due to her own insecurities, and doubt Sarah decided to take matters into her own hands. She caused her husband Abraham to go in to her own servant Hagar and conceive a child with her. The bible says that *"Sarah, Abraham's wife, took Hagar the Egyptian, her slave-girl, and gave her to her husband Abram as a wife. He went in to Hagar, and she conceived; and when she saw that she had conceived, she looked with contempt on her mistress"* Genesis 16:1-6.

How sad must this have been for Hagar, to be forced to have a child with her slave owner and then looked upon in contempt as if she had done something wrong. As the story goes Sarah later became so disgusted with Hagar and her son Ishmael that she banished them from the camp.

This is a true story for so many of us. We have been used in ways that were not our fault. People have sought to fulfill personal goals through using our bodies and then cast us aside as if we have done something wrong. It is painful. It is shameful. It causes us to ask God why he allowed this to happen to us, especially if the people who have caused the pain call themselves Christians.

To those things we do not know the answers; however we do know that God has not forgotten us. As Hagar and her son were in the desert they had used up all of their supplies that Abraham had given to them before he cast them away. Once everything was gone Hagar cried out to God to help her and her son who she knew was dying. In an answer to her prayer, the angel of God said to her *"What aileth thee, Hagar? Fear not; for God hath heard the voice of the lad where he is. Arise, lift up the lad, and hold him in thine hand; for I will make him a great nation. And God opened her eyes, and she saw a well of water; and she went, and filled the bottle with water, and gave the lad drink."*

When she was at the end of her rope and felt that no one cared about her even though she had been used, God showed her that he cared and would make her baby a great man.

God has not forgotten about those who are powerless and abused. He will provide a new well full of the living water in the midst of dry and desolate places in our lives. Fill up your skin with the new water and live again!

Day 3: Be Careful of Your Words

Often as we go through struggles in life, we say things that we later regret. We may speak too harshly to a loved one, friend, or co-worker, and later say to ourselves, "I sure wish I hadn't said that." Or what about the promises that we make to people? Sometimes they are made with the best of intentions, while other times we say whatever we have to in order to get ourselves out of bad situations.

A lot of times in our hurt and process of grieving we may say or do things toward God that tend to make us feel better like we have power over Him. For example "God, if you just let help me stop drinking, I'll go to church every day of the week for the rest of my life." Do you REALLY have plans on fulfilling this promise? What happens when God demands that you make good on your promises to Him, just as he makes good on His to you?

This was the story of Jephthah. Jephthah was an Israelite leader who was facing a very strong enemy in battle. In the vow of Jephthah, *Judges 11:1-11, 29-33* he promised God that in exchange for victory against his enemies, he would sacrifice the first thing he saw when he returned home. God gave Jephthah's army an incredible strength in order to defeat their opponents, and they returned home triumphant. Upon Jephthah's entry to his house, his daughter ran out to greet him. "*And Jephthah came to Mizpeh unto his house, and, behold, his daughter came out to meet him with timbrels and with dances: and she was his only child; beside her he had neither son nor daughter. And it came to pass, when he saw her, that he rent his clothes, and said, Alas, my daughter! Thou hast brought me very low, and thou art one of them that trouble me: for I have opened my mouth unto the LORD, and I cannot go back"* Judges 11: 34-35. Two months later, Jephthah sacrificed his daughter to the Lord.

Thank God for the sacrifice of his Son Jesus, so that we are no longer required to offer sacrifices of blood from animals or humans unto the Lord for our sins or in exchange or victories. However we must remember that we are still responsible for our words. The bible says that *death and life are in the power of the tongue* (Proverbs 18:21). We must speak things into our lives that we want for ourselves. Jephthah wanted the victory in battle so badly that he inadvertently lost his only child to get it. Was it worth it? Do you think he had to sacrifice his daughter for victory, or would his trust in God's salvation have resulted in the same outcome? How many times have we said and done things with one intention, only to gain horrible backlash?

God is faithful to us, he gives us second chances. Today use your second chance to think before you speak. Make promises to God that you can fulfill. He is faithful. He will always fulfill His promises to us.

Day 4: Looking for Love in All the Wrong Places

The story of Samson and Delilah is often told as one of a poor helpless man who was seduced by a horrible woman. However, I think it is a story that more of us can relate to if we're honest. Samson was a man who had been hurt by his past. His wife, child and father-in-law were killed by his enemies (Judges 15) and he was severely hurt by this. He promised to avenge the death of his family, and then went in to be with a prostitute (Judges 16:1).

After being with that prostitute, he met Delilah. The name Delilah from ancient translations seems to suggest that she too was of sexual prowess, and may have been a sacred temple prostitute. She was not mentioned as a wife of anyone, but yet she was engaged in sexual intercourse with a man from another place. This all seems very promiscuous to me!

So we have a man who's basically on the rebound with a woman who for some reason has given her body over for sex. This combination sounds like a no-win situation from the start. Samson was in a place of hurting. Delilah was also in a place of hurting, and was approached by the Philistine lords regarding finding out Samson's secret. *"And the lords of the Philistines came up unto her, and said unto her, Entice him, and see wherein his great strength lieth, and by what means* we may prevail against him, that we may bind him to afflict him: and we will give thee every one of us eleven hundred pieces of silver" Judges 16: 4-5.

Delilah did not love Samson. For her, this was a business venture. Likewise, we can ask ourselves if Samson really loved Delilah, or if he was just using her to fill the void left in his life by being a widower.

Though Delilah made a back room deal against Samson, he was not a complete victim. After all, she tried repeatedly to find out the secrets of his strength. Samson would tell her a bogus story, and each time after she thought to have weakened him she would cry, "The Philistines are upon us!" Why would he want to stay with a woman who was clearly setting him up for failure? Perhaps his place of hurt did not allow him to see the fact this woman was toxic to him. Perhaps her desire for acceptance in society which made her sell herself for money (instead of marrying) did not allow her to feel remorse for betraying a man who was in emotional distress.

Either way, the result was tragic. Samson, in his effort to make Delilah love him, divulged his most important secret. *"If I be shaven, then my strength will go from me, and I shall become weak, and be like any other man. And when Delilah saw that he had told her all his heart, she sent and called for the lords of the Philistines, saying, Come up this once, for he hath shewed me all his heart..."* Judges 16: 17-18. Delilah was paid her money and never heard of again. Both were used because of their own hurt. Both used each other. Delilah used Samson for money, Samson used Delilah to make him feel loved.

Are you using someone to fill the pain you have felt because of being mistreated? Are you being used by someone else? Today, ask God to fill the voids in your life with the fruit of the spirit. Seek to serve and be used by Him. He will not betray you. He will not seek to destroy your strength, but instead increase it. Today, allow the love of God to be what you pursue, and what you show others. Stop looking for love in all the wrong places.

Day 5: Used but Still "Used"

How many times have we heard the term "used" to describe a woman or man who has engaged in sexual promiscuity? Even when someone is abused, it seems the term still comes from the victim's own mouth as though they have no merit or value because of what has been done to their bodies. What does this term really mean? The basic dictionary definition of used is: *previously owned, exploited*. Where is the shame in that? If a body was previously owned or exploited, surely it is not the fault of the victim.

Rahab was used, repeatedly and on purpose. In a society where purity and virginity was valued above all things, she was a prostitute. The bible gives us an indication that the living quarters was close to the gates of the city, which meant that men coming and going into the city of Jericho could pass by her place, meet her for cheap sex, and go about their business. She must have encountered all sorts of travelers and likely diseased and dirty men as well. But somehow, out of all of the possible places for the Israeli spies to hide in Jericho, they chose the house of the "ho". *Then Joshua son of Nun sent two men secretly from Shittim as spies, saying, 'Go, view the land, especially Jericho.' So they went, and entered the house of a prostitute whose name was Rahab, and spent the night there"* Joshua 2:1.

Why this house? Why would God to use choose a woman who had allowed herself to be used by men? She was thrown away by society and seen as nothing, because she did not keep herself pure and wait until marriage for sex. Yet, she was close enough to the important people of the land that spies could go into her house and hear what was going on. This seems to suggest that perhaps some of the men in her life who were using her for sex were also people in power within the city government.

This may allow us to better understand why it was so easy for Rahab to make a deal with the spies to save only her family when the city was destroyed. She had been exploited. She had been used by those around her, but when the time came to make a change, she did what she needed to in order to better her situation. According to Joshua 2: 12-14, there was a verbal exchange between Rahab and the men after she had hidden them in her home. *" Now therefore, I pray you, swear unto me by the LORD, since I have shewed you kindness, that ye will also shew kindness unto my father's house, and give me a true token: And that ye will save alive my father, and my mother, and my brethren, and my sisters, and all that they have, and deliver our lives from death. And the men answered her, Our life for yours, if ye utter not this our business. And it shall be, when the LORD hath given us the land, that we will deal kindly and truly with thee."*

When it was time to follow God's plan, though she had been "used" by man, she still allowed herself to be used by God,

22

and in exchange He saved her life. Today, do not allow the past exploitations to hinder God from using you. You are worth saving in God's eyes. Leave those behind who have exploited you, and give yourself over to God. Allow him to abide with you, listen to His plan for how to rescue you from where you are and what you have done. He will save your life!

Day 6: When No One Believes You (or believes IN you)

Joseph was a dreamer. He was loved by his father Israel because he was his youngest child and had been conceived at an old age. The bible says in Genesis 37 that *"Israel loved Joseph more than all his children, because he was the son of his old age: and he made him a coat of many colours. And when his brethren saw that their father loved him more than all his brethren, they hated him, and could not speak peaceably unto him ."*

Israel was clearly playing favorites and Joseph's brothers could not take this treatment. They finally became fed up with him and his dreams about being a leader over them and threw him into a pit. The brothers took his beautiful coat, stained it with the blood of an animal, and convinced Israel that his beloved baby boy had been attacked and killed. While Israel grieved his loss, Joseph was sold into slavery to Egyptians. All of this happened to Joseph at just 17 years old.

In Egypt, Joseph was a good slave, so much so that he was quickly elevated to the role of living and working in Potiphar's house. Joseph ran the house so well that according to Genesis 39:6 Potiphar really did not know or have to concern himself with what was going on and only cared about what he would eat. That left one person inside of the house unattended to, and that was Potiphar's wife who had developed a lust for Joseph. *"And it came to pass after these things, that his master's wife cast her eyes upon Joseph; and she said, Lie with me"* Genesis 39:7.

As if Joseph had not been traumatized enough by being betrayed by his own brothers and sold into slavery in a foreign land, he was now being sexually harassed by his boss' wife. Joseph remained true to his own character and refused the offer. This angered the wife, and after multiple attempts, she finally grabbed his coat and falsely accused him of trying to rape her. Of course, since he was a slave, no one believed him, and he was thrown in jail.

What do you do when no one believes you? When you're just trying to live out your dreams and live the life God has called you to, but someone takes advantage of you and your sexuality, and somehow YOU are called the aggressor? You may be thrown into a jail of being ostracized by friends and family. You may be thrown into a jail of your own mind and thoughts, questioning whether you actually did something wrong. You may be thrown into a physical jail because of false accusations. No matter which kind of jail you find yourself in, know that God is with you.

It was not fair. A grown woman took advantage of a teenage boy and lusted after him when he was in a captive state. But Joseph stayed true to himself. Despite his circumstances, he used who he WAS to get where God wanted him to be. Though no one else believed him, Joseph believed in himself and better yet, he believed in God. He knew that the dreams God had given to him would eventually come to pass and get him out of that mess. He did not get out of jail through lying and scheming, he got out through dreaming! God has placed something inside of you that you may feel is useless. We have been used and abused because of the lusts of those who were supposed to be watching over us. But God always knows and believes us, and still wants us to keep our dreams alive. Use those dreams to set yourself free from whatever jail you may find yourself in.

Day 7: A Super Model

Have you ever watched a beauty pageant or seen supermodels on TV or in magazines, and thought to yourself "If I looked like that, life would be great!"? Many times our personal sense of self worth is attached to our outward appearance. But what happens when what we look like on the outside is not what others would consider beautiful? What lengths are you willing to go to in order to gain the love and validation you feel you deserve when no one is really even giving you a second look?

This was the story of Leah. She was the oldest daughter of Laban, brother of Rachel. After tricking his own father Isaac into giving him an inheritance, Jacob went away from his homeland to live with his uncle Laban. He had travelled far and was tired when he arrived at a well, where he met Rachel. *"And it came to pass, when Jacob saw Rachel the daughter of Laban his mother's brother, and the sheep of Laban his mother's brother, that Jacob went near, and rolled the stone from the well's mouth, and watered the flock of Laban his mother's brother. And Jacob kissed Rachel, and lifted up his voice, and wept"* Genesis 29: 10-11. Jacob was overcome with emotion when he met Rachel and cried after he kissed her. That was truly love at first sight!

Jacob went to Rachel's father Laban and made an arrangement with him that he would work for seven years in order to marry her. At the end of the seven years, Jacob discussed with Laban that he had fulfilled his obligation and was ready for his bride. The bible says that Laban held a feast for the bridal ceremony and served much wine to Jacob. When Jacob had quite a bit to drink, Laban sent in Leah his oldest daughter fully veiled and clothes as Jacob's bride. Since Jacob was intoxicated, and his bride was hiding her face, he consummated the marriage, not knowing that he had been tricked.

Imagine Jacob's fury when he discovered that his uncle had tricked him after all of his hard work! Genesis 29: 25 says *"and he said to Laban, What is this thou hast done unto me? did not I serve with thee for Rachel? wherefore then hast thou beguiled me?"* Laban explained that in his country the eldest daughter had to be married first, so Jacob had to work another seven years for Rachel whom he loved.

It is easy to place ourselves in Leah's shoes. She was not the pretty girl in the family. Her own father validated her sense of worthlessness by tricking someone into marrying her, and now even her new husband was disgusted by her. But God did not overlook her inner pain and exclusion based on her looks. In fact, the bible tells us that *"when the LORD saw that Leah was hated, he opened her womb"* Genesis 29: 31. Rachel, the more beautiful sister remained barren, but Leah had three sons; Reuben, Simeon and Judah. The lineage of our savior Jesus Christ began with an "Ugly Betty"!

The bible says that *"Man looks at the outward appearance, but God looks on the heart."* I Samuel 16:7. Today, focus on your heart. Is it right toward God? Do you spend as much time lifting up your voice in praise to God as you do fixing your hair and make-up? Do you devote as much time in prayer as looking for the latest trends? Leah was treated badly because she was not beautiful, but God took a person that others may have looked away from, and through her bloodline saved the world. He has a special purpose for each of us. Our physical looks do not matter to God. Through his blood He can make each and every one of us a SUPER model!

Day 8: All Up In Your Business

For me, there have been times when I just wanted to be left alone to get through my issues. People who love me and are close to me would ask me questions about the abuse, and why I acted out in certain ways. They always said that they were just trying to understand me better, but I felt like they were just trying to be in my business. You may have felt like this before. It's hard to explain to someone who has not been abused the pain that you feel. Many people don't understand why you would want to just block parts of your life out, and keep living like certain events never happened.

That's probably how the woman in John chapter four felt. Jesus was at a well when he met a Samaritan woman who was getting water. Jesus asked the woman to give Him a drink. Immediately the woman was defensive because she was a Samaritan and looked down upon by the Jews. She basically was like "Why are YOU asking ME for anything?" Jesus replied to her that if she knew who He was, she would ask Him for "living water". She was curious and asked Him about the "living water". Jesus responded by telling her to go and get her husband and come back. She said *"I have no husband"* John 4:17a. Jesus replied *"Thou hast well said, I have no husband: For thou hast had five husbands; and he whom thou now hast is not thy husband: in that saidst thou truly"* John 4:17b-18.

Jesus was all in her business! He called her out by telling her that not only had she been married five times, but she was shacking up with a man at the time. Now, most of us, if we had that kind of information on a person would quickly get on our cell phones, computers, or PDAs to begin the gossip mill, but Jesus was not that way. He perceived that this woman was looking for something to fill a void she had inside. She was a five time divorcee in a society that valued only one marriage. She was living with a man who was not her husband. She was from an ethnicity that was not respected in the land. She was probably just trying to block some of the bad stuff out.

Even though Jesus knew all of her business, He did not put her down. In fact, He didn't even ask for a play-by-play of what happened with marriages one thru five, or why she was living with man number six. He already knew all of this! He knew that for a woman to behave in this way, she had to be hurting. This is why He offered her the "living water". He did not judge her He only told her to go and get others and tell them that she had met Christ. She went into the city saying *"Come, see a man, which told me all things that ever I did:* John 4: 29a. And John 4:39 says that *"And many of the Samaritans of that city believed on him for the saying of the woman, which testified."*

This is what God wants from us today. He knows what has happened to us. He knows all of the harmful and damaging things we have done to our bodies and maybe even other

31

people as a result of our hurt. He knows what people may be saying about us behind our backs. He knows that we are defensive because of being ridiculed. He knows that we want to forget the past ever happened and just focus on the present. Unlike people, He does not want to focus on those things He wants us to focus on Him. An important part of this scripture is the fact that people in the city believed in Jesus because of the woman's testimony. Today, do not be ashamed to share your testimony. God has done great things for you. You may be in the process of deliverance, but you can still share your encounter with God. He loves you. He knows all your business, but only wants to focus on one thing, HIS LOVE.

Day 9: Dead, but Not Done

How many times have you thought to yourself "It's too late for me, I've made such a mess of my life that I can't possibly do or be anything successful now!" I know at various times in my own life, I sat down and thought about the time I wasted in college, hanging out with friends instead of studying. Or the years I wasted in dead end relationships with guys who I knew didn't really love me. I was spending my life trying to use people and things to replace the spot in my heart that was just crying out to be free of pain. Sometimes I have met people who have been through situations like mine who may have turned to drugs, sex or alcohol as a method of self-medication. The damage they have done to their bodies seems so severe that they feel there is no hope for them. Is there? How does Jesus feel about people who are essentially dead?

John chapter 11 helps us understand Jesus' feelings toward people who have "died" for one reason or another. The chapter begins with the story of a man named Lazarus, who had two sisters (Mary and Martha). The passage tells us that Jesus loved Lazarus, and he was sick. His sisters sent someone to let Jesus know that Lazarus was very ill, and Jesus didn't go to Lazarus for two days! That would seem so cruel to me. However, Jesus said something very important to those who sent for him, *"This sickness is not unto death, but for the glory of God..."*John 11:4. This statement suggests that Jesus knew Lazarus would die, but somehow God would get the glory in the situation. After two days, Jesus journeyed to Lazarus' home and sure enough, he was dead and had been in the grave for four days. His sister Martha was angry with the Lord and blamed him saying *"Lord, if thou hadst been here, my brother had not died"* John 11:21. Jesus immediately told her that he was the resurrection and the life, and though Lazarus was currently dead, if she would believe in Him, He had the power to make Lazarus come back to life. She did believe, and Jesus called her brother back from the dead.

Jesus has the power to bring all of us back from any situation that has killed us inside. Though we do not know why bad things have happened to us in the first place, we can take encouragement from Jesus' words in John 11:4. Whatever situations we have faced are not unto death but for the glory of God. Lazarus could have been healed by Jesus speaking the Word over him from a far. He could have left as soon as the message arrived that Lazarus was ill. Why the Lord let Lazarus get all the way down to death is not quite clear, however what is clear is that in the end, he did not stay dead. There was an important element here, it is called belief that Jesus could raise a corpse buried for four days and restore him back to his family.

Today, you are not physically dead, but maybe your spirit is. Maybe the trials of life and your pain have caused you to bury yourself in work, anger, material possessions, food, drugs, alcohol, sex, or abusive relationships. Jesus has arrived. He knows all about what you are going through, and like Lazarus, He loves you too. He is just waiting for you to reach out to Him and let Him know you need Him. The question is do you believe that He has the power to raise you from your place of death? Are you ready to be free of your grave and once again walk among the living? Being dead is easy. You have to do nothing but lay there in the ground, but being alive takes real work. He will raise you. Do you believe?

Day 10: Do Not Follow Your Father's Footsteps

The statistics of those who have been abused as children are staggering. For years, it seemed that crimes of incest, or molestation were not even discussed. There are many who have suffered in silence for decades. Often times, individuals that have abused others, were abused as children themselves. In many interviews with child predators, or those who have sexually abused someone, the accused confess that they had been victimized as children, and were only repeating actions committed against them as children. Perhaps you come from a long line of abusers. It may seem that having bad things happen to you and those you love is somehow in your DNA. Maybe no one in your family has ever done anything positive. No matter what has happened or where you come from, God wants you to know that nothing you were born into limits your ability to change history for future generations.

In the book of second Kings, we are introduced to a young boy named Josiah. This child came from two generations of biblical "thugs". The family had started as a God fearing one when they first became the rulers of their land. However, at some point, Josiah's grandfather Manasseh decided to turn the land away from worshipping God, and they began idol worship. Manasseh turned a once holy temple into a place where idols now lived, and became a notorious murderer. *"Moreover, Manasseh also shed so much innocent blood that he filled Jerusalem from end to end—besides the sin that he had caused Judah to commit, so that they did evil in the eyes of the LORD"* 2 Kings 21:16. Josiah's father Amon continued the tradition of idolatry and also disobeyed God *"He did evil in the eyes of the LORD, as his father Manasseh had done. He walked in all the ways of his father; he worshiped the idols his father had worshiped, and bowed down to them. He forsook the LORD, the God of his fathers, and did not walk in the way of the LORD." 2 Kings 21: 20-22.*

King Amon was assassinated, which left Josiah to reign as king at the age of eight. As a boy, he had the opportunity to follow the path that his father and grandfather had prepared for him. After all, as hard core infamous criminals, there was certainly a level of fear than they had instilled in the inhabitants of the kingdom. I'm sure people knew not to mess with that family or risk losing their lives! But despite all of the horrible things that Josiah had likely witnessed, heard about, and possibly experienced from his family, the bible says in 2 Kings 22:2 that *"he did that which was right in the sight of the LORD..."*. At age 26, he took the money that was previously used to turn the temple into a house of pagan worship, and restored it to a place where the Lord would be praised.

Being born into the right family can be a great blessing, being born into the wrong family can be a great curse. Who determines which family we are born into? We do. When we accept Jesus into our hearts as our Lord and personal savior, we are born into the family of God. It doesn't matter where you came from, who birthed you, what they did to you or others. Once we accept God's love, we are His children and are to act like Him. We can no longer blame our lineage for mistakes we make in life. Today, accept God's adoption plan for your life. Cry out "Abba Father" to Him. Allow Him to free you from your natural heritage and let the Blood of Jesus become your inheritance.

Day 11: Called Out But Not Cast Out

Have you ever watched the TV show "Cheaters"? There is usually a man or woman who suspects that their partner or spouse is seeing another person. A private investigator follows the unfaithful person for a few days, and finally catches the couple in the act as proof of infidelity. There is a huge confrontation, usually followed by hurt, questions and finally a breakup.

There is a similar story in the bible in John chapter eight. Jesus had come down from the Mount of Olives and was teaching a crowd when the Pharisees brought a woman to him who they claim had been involved in an affair, *"And the scribes and Pharisees brought unto him a woman taken in adultery; and when they had set her in the midst, They say unto him, Master, this woman was taken in adultery, in the very act" John 8:3-4*. They wanted her stoned for her act. Why would they do this in front of the crowd? If they were really concerned with helping her and bringing her to Jesus for her to be saved, why not just hold her in the temple and wait until the lesson was over? Furthermore, if she was caught in the "very act", where was the man that she was with?

Isn't it amazing how some people set their sights on YOU and only YOU? They spend hours a day worrying about what you're doing, where you're going, and how you're living your life. They never take into account the other characters in your life that may have caused you to get to the place where you are today. If the woman was caught in adultery, why was she singled out and all of her business put in the street like that? Were the officials of the temple really trying to help her, or were they set on humiliating her?

The beautiful part in the story is where Jesus says NOTHING to her accusers. He didn't ask where she was, who she was with, what she was wearing, NOTHING! He simply bends down and starts writing something on the ground. Then He gets up, asks who has never sinned to throw the first stone at the lady, and starts writing again. "*But Jesus stooped down, and with his finger wrote on the ground, as though he heard them not. So when they continued asking him, he lifted up himself, and said unto them, He that is without sin among you, let him first cast a stone at her. And again he stooped down, and wrote on the ground*" John 8:6-8. What was Jesus writing? Perhaps the names of those in the crowd who had also committed adultery but not been caught. Maybe He was writing down a list of secret sins that others had engaged in all by themselves, and thought nobody knew. Whatever it was, the whole crowd dispersed and left the woman alone with Jesus.

Then He looked at her and asked her where her accusers were. She replied that there was no one left. Then he showed his compassion toward her "*And Jesus said unto her, Neither do I condemn thee: go, and sin no more*" John 8:10.

40

It doesn't matter what "dirt" people think they have on us, and how they try to embarrass us in front of others as we walk in this new life. Jesus does not condemn us. He does not even engage in long and drawn out conversations about the drama. He simply tells us to "Go and sin no more." That should be our focus today. Not to spend time worrying about who is trying to keep us boxed in to what we once were and to classify us in the old place. We should instead focus on the love of Christ that does not condemn us, but turns the focus to His forgiveness for all, and tells us to "Sin no more."

Day 12: Heads Up

In my hurt I know that I have said and done many things to people that I loved dearly. Sometimes looking back at the instances, I have felt completely justified, saying to myself, "Well, they don't understand me and my background." And it is very true. People who have been abused by others, especially as kids come with a certain set of insecurities, relational disorders, and self-esteem concerns that most of the general public cannot relate to. We see ourselves through the eyes of a person who has survived something heinous, yet we cannot let ourselves rest. We usually do not trust people, and are often on the offensive so that we do not find ourselves in a position of having to be defended. It is often called the old "chip on the shoulder". We are ready to react to anyone, or anything that threatens the walls we have built around us.

When we are finally ready to let the walls go and really open our hearts to Christ so that He can heal us, there are times when others may not understand. Have you ever heard someone say "I can't believe SHE has the nerve to be doing THAT after everything she's done." You may want to respond "It's none of your business." And you are right! God tells us that if we confess our sins to Him, He is faithful and just to forgive us of our sins and cleanse us of all unrighteousness. I John 1:9

Romans 8:1 says *"There is therefore now no condemnation to them who are in Christ Jesus. Who walk not after the flesh, but after the Spirit."* This means that once we fully decide to make Jesus the Lord of our lives and leave the flesh behind that our sins are not held against us. Paul says *"I am crucified with Christ, nevertheless I live, yet not I, but Christ liveth in me. And the life that I now live in the flesh, I live by the faith of the Son of God who loved me and gave himself for me"* Galatians 2:20. When we put the flesh to death, we live day-to-day by our faith in Jesus who loved us and gave himself for us.

People may hold your sins against you for years and years, but God does not. In fact, he doesn't even hold grudges for 24 hours, because the Word tells us that His mercy unto us is renewed every morning. Lamentations 3: 22-24 says *"It is of the LORD'S mercies that we are not consumed, because his compassions fail not. They are new every morning: great is thy faithfulness. The LORD is my portion, saith my soul; therefore will I hope in him."*

Every single morning God gives us a second chance. You may have to clean up some messes of your past, but hold your head high. God has forgiven you. He does not condemn you. Live day-by-day relying on your faith in Jesus Christ to reveal to others the newness that He has given within. Hold your head up. You are free!

Day 13: Taking One For the Team

When I was abused, I had just started junior high school. I was 12 years old, and the oldest of 4 kids. I was a good student, and great daughter. I was obedient, reliable, and always got good grades. I enjoyed helping my mother care for my younger siblings, and felt like I would do anything to keep them safe. That's how my abuser got to me. My abuser convinced me that if I said anything about being molested that my siblings would be sent to foster care and worse things could happen to them. I loved my siblings so much that I agreed within myself to take the pain, shame and guilt at the hands of my father rather than endanger their lives.

This story is not new. There is a similar one found in I Samuel 20, where we can observe the love between Jonathan and David. This is the same David who killed Goliath and became a hero in the land. Somehow King Saul became filled with jealousy toward David and conspired to kill him. Jonathan was King Saul's son and David's best friend. He could not understand his father's rage toward David and vowed to help David get away from Saul. Jonathan came up with a plan for David to sneak away during a very important feast. No one ever missed this feast, so David's absence was a big deal for King Saul, and he asked Jonathan where David was. Jonathan did not want to reveal his friend's location since he knew it would probably cause him to be killed, so he took the blame for everything. He told Saul that he had given permission for David to miss the feast and go be with his family.

The bible says that after that Saul's anger was kindled against Jonathan. He embarrassed him in front of everyone at the ceremony, *"he said unto him, Thou son of the perverse rebellious woman, do not I know that thou hast chosen the son of Jesse to thine own confusion"* I Samuel 20:30. Saul cursed Jonathan, his own son, called his mother names, and told him that as long as David was alive he would never prosper. David was able to escape the kingdom with Jonathan's help and become King of Israel. We never hear about Jonathan again until his death in battle, when David writes the beautiful "Song of the Bow" to discuss his love for a true friend (I Samuel 1:18).

It is my prayer that this story is as encouraging for you as it was for me. After all, I felt that I had sacrificed so much and had endured humiliation to protect those that I loved. Perhaps you have had the same experience. As victims of sexual abuse we often do not tell because of thinking about the feelings of others and the reactions of loved ones when they find out what we've been through. It is a hard place to be. Like Jonathan, we are innocent, and we also took the abuse to protect others who are innocent.

Today God wants us to know that He has not forgotten. When David ran away from Saul, we heard nothing more about him until his death. Yet today the story of Jonathan and David is known to be one of the greatest stories of friendship in history. God has not forgotten you. Those you have protected have not forgotten you. It may seem like no one cares, but there will come a day when everyone in your life will know what a hero you are. They will know your story of bravery and love. There will be a "Song of the Bow" with your name on it, because you too are a hero!

Day 14: Just Take It

When I started to create a new life, I sometimes had periods of wondering. I wondered why I had been abused in the first place. I wondered why I had created and felt such comfort as I shielded myself from pain by keeping others out. I wondered about the loss of certain friends and family who I felt would do nothing to really help me start over. I had to give up a lot. I had to start from scratch. I put up a brave front, but inside of myself I really didn't know if I had what it took to be a different person who only looked ahead. It would take a lot to be someone who just trusted God even though I didn't have answers to my questions. It was a daunting task, but I somehow knowing the story of Job helped me feel that I was up to it.

In Job chapter one we are introduced to a man who is described as "blameless and upright; he feared God and shunned evil. He was a wealthy man with seven thousand sheep, three thousand camels, five thousand oxen, servants, seven sons and three daughters. He had EVERYTHING! The devil went to God looking for a person to attack. God had so much confidence in his relationship with Job that he knew no matter what the devil did to him, he would still trust in Him. Job was majorly attacked. First all of his sheep, and servants except for one were killed. While he was receiving the news about that calamity, someone came to him and told him that all of his children had been killed. Job's response *"Then Job arose, and rent his mantle, and shaved his head, and fell down upon the ground, and worshipped, And said, Naked came I out of my mother's womb, and naked shall I return thither: the LORD gave, and the LORD hath taken away; blessed be the name of the LORD"* Job 1:20-21.

Job's response would not have been one to which many of us can relate. Job lost everything, tore his clothes shaved his head and worshipped God. He was cursed with many more things, so much so that his friends were beginning to think that maybe he had done something wrong, but in everything that he went through, he would not give up on God. The whole book is filled with conversations between Job and his friends, as they kept trying to convince him that God had given up on him. He refused to believe it, and continued to bless God even as he questioned why so many bad things had happened to him. He also prayed for his friends who no longer believed in him.

In the final book of Job, chapter 42 verse 10 we see that *"And the LORD turned the captivity of Job, when he prayed for his friends: also the LORD gave Job twice as much as he had before."* The book of Job ends with Job having fourteen thousand sheep, six thousand camels, a thousand oxen and female donkeys. He also got ten children, seven sons and three daughters. His daughters were the most beautiful in the land.

While we don't have answers for the bad things that happen to us, we do have answers for how to handle them. There is nothing wrong with crying, questioning or being sad. But in everything that we do, we must continue to worship God. He is the only one who truly has the power to restore us. Just take it. There is glory on the other side of your pain!

Who Am I?

A woman?

A wife?

A mother?

A daughter?

A sister?

A friend?

A lover?

Am I all of these things?

Am I none of these things?

Who can help me find me?

Is there a lost and found for souls?

Where do you find a soul taken from its rightful
owner, used and cast aside?

Where is it found?

Who can help me find ME?

Day 15: Somebody's Waiting For You

In our daily walk with God and making an effort to fully repent from all that we have done, be healed of all that has been done to us, and live our lives as new creatures in Christ, we often have moments when we feel that there is no one who will support us in our walk. It seems that there are so many people who spent lots of time bringing up the past, that few care to even try to live with us in the present, and even fewer look toward the future.

In Acts 9, there is a story of a man who had to change his life. Saul of Tarsus was a notorious man who was known throughout the land for killing Christians. He was very powerful in this endeavor, and would even go into synagogues demanding to know the names of men and women who worshipped there so that he could take them as prisoners and kill them. He was a cold blooded killer! One day, when he was on his way to a city where he would find more Christians to hurt, God knocked him off of his donkey and spoke to him. He asked Saul why he was persecuting Him, blinded him, and gave him instructions on what to do with his life. *"And he trembling and astonished said, Lord, what wilt thou have me to do? And the Lord said unto him, Arise, and go into the city, and it shall be told thee what thou must do."* Acts 9:6

As Saul was on his way to Damascus, God spoke to a man named Ananais to let him know that Saul was coming, and that he should lay hands on him to help him regain his sight. Can you imagine Ananais' terror? God as not only asking him to pray for a known killer, but to personally go to this man and lay hands on him? The bible tells us that Ananais was afraid, *"Then Ananias answered, Lord, I have heard by many of this man, how much evil he hath done to thy saints at Jerusalem..."* Acts 9:13. But the Lord reassured Ananais that He had changed Saul's heart and that he was now called to do great things in the name of Jesus. So Ananais obeyed God, laid hands on Saul, Saul regained his sight, immediately joined the disciples, and after a few days began preaching about the Lord. *"And Ananias went his way, and entered into the house; and putting his hands on him said, Brother Saul, the Lord, even Jesus, that appeared unto thee in the way as thou camest, hath sent me, that thou mightest receive thy sight, and be filled with the Holy Ghost. And immediately there fell from his eyes as it had been scales: and he received sight forthwith, and arose, and was baptized"* Acts 9:17-18.

God has someone waiting on you too. No matter what you have done in the past, when you make the decision to turn your life completely over to God, He hears you and prepares a support system of believers to help you. He has already touched the heart of a person who knows that you are really ready to make a change. There is a person who will lay their hands, on you, pray for you, and help you regain your sight so that you can see yourself as God sees you. By having your sight back, you will also be able to have a "vision". This vision is the plan that God has for your life, and your purpose on this Earth. Today, allow God to reveal to you who is waiting for you. Know that He has already planned this encounter or place in your life where someone would help you regain your sight. Wait for Him. Know that very soon, your vision will be restored.

Day 16: Hide Your Baby

After I decided to really turn my spirit, heart, mind, and body over to God I had to make some decisions. Would I still be friends with the same people? Would I be able to stay in my marriage with a husband who was married to the old me? Who should I share my pain and transformation with? Was I prepared for the many questions from people who may start off by saying "You changed." When I really became serious about being new in Christ, I went into hiding. I disconnected my old email and social networking accounts, I stayed off the internet, I didn't talk on the phone to anyone but close friends and family. I felt that it was a very serious case of a life and death matter!

The story of Moses begins in much of the same way. The Pharaoh of Egypt became jealous of the Israelite slaves, the way they continued to reproduce, and grow in number. He demanded that all midwives who delivered Hebrew boys kill them by drowning immediately after birth. *"And he said, When ye do the office of a midwife to the Hebrew women, and see them upon the stools; if it be a son, then ye shall kill him: but if it be a daughter, then she shall live"* Exodus 1:16. Moses' mother Jochebed was a God fearing woman who refused to let her son be taken away from her by death. When he was born she hid him in the house for three months. Once he got too big to hide in the house she devised a plan to save his life. Jochebed made a basket for her son and placed him into the river praying that someone would find him and care for him. She sent Miriam, Moses' sister to watch over the basket. The Pharaoh's daughter happened to be bathing in the river at the same time the basket came along. She decided to keep baby Moses. Miriam who had been watching the whole thing suggested that a nurse be found for the baby. The Pharaoh's daughter agreed, and Miriam went to get her mother Jochebed. The Pharaoh's daughter was so happy to have a Hebrew nurse for her son that she agreed to pay Jochebed to raise her own baby! *"And Pharaoh's daughter said unto her, Take this child away, and nurse it for me, and I will give thee thy wages. And the woman took the child, and nursed it"* Exodus 2:9.

This is a lesson for all of us. We have been through terrible trauma that sought to kill our dreams and destroy our purpose and destiny. We have to hide the infancy of those things God has placed inside of us. Everyone will not be happy about the changes that you are making in life. Some people prefer you when you are down and dependent. They thrive on your inability to fend for yourself and have security in who you are. Some people take advantage of others when they are at their worst. These individuals will only seek to kill the new life God has given you.

You have to hide your baby. God will show you how to protect your dream from demise. He will reveal to you how to cover it and keep it safe until it is time to display it to the world. Today, trust God's plan for your new life. Just like

Pharaoh's daughter, there is a person that God has strategically placed in your path who will help you nurture your new life. You will not have to give it up forever, you will not have it destroyed, and in fact YOU will be there to see it grow into everything God has intended for it to be.

God took Moses from a baby hiding in a basket, to the one who led thousands of people out of captivity. He has a great plan for your new life too. It is precious cargo. Hide that baby!

Day 17: Protected for Purpose

Sometimes in life as I have accomplished various things, I have stopped and thought to myself "God, why me?" There have been so many people that I have encountered who have experienced abuse worse than mine, some less traumatic, or even no abuse at all, who have made terrible choices in life. I have met people on the streets, homeless, into drugs and prostitution. You may have also been into some of those things, but you are here now, reading devotionals and getting yourself right with God. Have you ever wondered why He allowed you to live long enough to turn your life around?

Jonah was a man who was chosen by God for a specific task. He was told by God to go into a city called Nineveh and preach because the city was very sinful. Jonah did not feel that he could do this task. The bible says in Jonah 1:3, *"But Jonah rose up to flee unto Tarshish from the presence of the LORD, and went down to Joppa; and he found a ship going to Tarshish."* The New International Version of the same verse says, *"But Jonah ran away from the LORD and headed for Tarshish"* Jonah ran away from God.

How many times have you been in a church service and heard a song or sermon that touched your heart and spirit, but you refused to change because you really didn't want to accept the fact that God had a purpose for your life? You were running from God. Jonah was on a mission to get away from God and avoid going to Nineveh to preach to the sinful city. Once he got onto a boat and tried to just be normal and go to another city, there was a huge storm. The men on board knew that God was upset about something, and Jonah confessed that it was him. In an effort to save the entire ship the sailors threw him overboard. God didn't let him drown though, a big fish swallowed him whole and he spent 3 days in the fish's belly.

What an encouraging story of God's protection for us! Even when we set out to disobey God on purpose, he still protects us and gives us a second chance. Jonah cried out to God in the belly of the fish *"When my soul fainted within me I remembered the LORD: and my prayer came in unto thee, into thine holy temple" Jonah 2: 7.* God saved him, and caused the fish to vomit Jonah onto dry land. He had purposed in his heart that he would do the Will of God. The third chapter of Jonah begins with *"And the word of the LORD came unto Jonah the second time..."* God reminded Jonah of what He wanted him to do, and where to go in order to preach the Word. This time Jonah did not run away from God, but ran towards the plan for his life.

What has God protected you **for**? Perhaps you have an eloquent speaking voice, and have been saved from abuse to tell others about how to overcome what has happened to them without living in fear or shame. Or maybe you can share a word with survivors through song. Are you an excellent writer who can write articles, or books to encourage people? There are also those who have loving hearts and would do well as volunteers in shelters and other rehabilitation centers. Whatever it is, know that God protected you for a reason. No matter where you have been and how bad it may have seemed, you were always covered and protected by God. Today, open your heart and spirit to the possibilities that God has for your life. Be willing to explore all that He has for you, and ways that your testimony can serve to help others find Christ. After all, He protected you for a purpose!

Day 18: Making Your Life Count

I work for a large corporation, and every so often there are announcements of retirees who have passed away. There will be a short write up about the person's life. There is information about where he or she went to school, settled, what they did for the company, how many years of service they gave, and by whom they are survived. In reading those passages I often think to myself what full lives these people have lived. I wonder if they set out to live lives that benefitted others, or if it just happened by chance. I also think to myself about my life and sometimes pause to reflect on what others might say about me when it is time for me to go home with God.

Dorcas (translated Tabitha Acts chapter 9) was a seamstress who was known throughout community because she was a, *"woman full of good works and almsdeeds which she did"* Acts 9:36. Almsdeeds is an old word for charity work. The bible says that Dorcas was "full of good works". What proof do we have that she was full of these good things for others and not just doing them to make herself look good in front of others? When she died people immediately went to get the apostle Peter to pray over her. There was a sense of urgency that something had to be done about her passing. Upon arrival, the text tells us that, *"all the widows stood by him weeping, and shewing the coats and garments which Dorcas made, while she was with them"* Acts 9:39. In that society, a woman without a husband had no rights, financial, societal or political covering. Widows were essentially nobodies! Yet, Dorcas had made coats and garments for them. We can assume that without husbands to work and provide for them, the women had little to no money, but somehow they had been given multiple items that they could show Peter when he arrived.

Peter was definitely able to see how important this seamstress was in her community. Her life's work reflected a woman who was selfless and caring, looking out for those who were less fortunate and likely forgotten. Without hesitation, he *"kneeled down, and prayed; and turning him to the body said, Tabitha, arise. And she opened her eyes: and when she saw Peter, she sat up"* Acts 9:40.

What are you doing? How do you make your life count? As badly as you think your life is, there is someone less fortunate than you. The passage does not tell us that Tabitha gave large sums of money to these widows, she made clothes for them. She had a skill. She did not make excuses, but used what God had given her to be a blessing to others. I find it interesting that this seamstress was so important to her community that the apostle Peter traveled to find her and brought her back to life. This is what God wants from all of us. Not, excuses-USES!

Today, challenge yourself to find a new way to make your life count. Everyone has problems it is a fact of life. But today focus less on yourself and more on using the talent that God has placed inside of you to be a blessing to others. He has raised us all from the dead; dead end living, destruction to our bodies and spirits, dead relationships, dead futures. Now let's take every day to live for Him. Reach out to those in need. Make your life count so much that when you are gone others will have proof of your good works. Today, "Arise" and get to work. Those less fortunate in our world are waiting for you.

Day 19: Stepping Out of Your Comfort Zone

I know that ever since I shared the horrible secret about being molested with my friends and family, I tried many times to turn over a new leaf. I was going to be less angry, more compassionate, slower to react to bad things, and not turn off movies that had abuse in them to show everyone that I was really over it. But time after unsuccessful time, I would somehow resort back to my same place of anger, resentment, and mistrust. This is a place known as my comfort zone. It is not necessarily a comfortable place for me, because I did not like feeling angry or resentful or not trusting others, but it is comfortable because not matter how bad and dark it was, I knew what to expect.

Many of us have comfort zones of some sort. Perhaps they are relationships with family members or loved ones. Often we are in commitments with people who are toxic to us, but do not leave because being unhappy may seem better than being alone. Others may find comfort in physical addictions to things such as drugs, alcohol, or even food. These vices may harm us in ways that will eventually kill us, but not having those means facing hurt, fear, and having to take a chance by trusting that we will not be traumatized again.

I believe this was what Peter faced in Matthew 14. The disciples had just finished watching Jesus perform the miracle of the fives loaves and two fish being used to feed over 5,000 people, when they were traveling in a boat to another location. In the middle of the night they saw what they thought was a ghost walking toward the boat. Peter thought he recognized the figure as Jesus and said, *"Lord, if it be thou, bid me come unto thee on the water"* Matthew 14: 28. Jesus responded to Peter, *"And he said, Come. And when Peter was come down out of the ship, he walked on the water, to go to Jesus"* Matthew 14:29. Peter was a fisherman by trade, and that boat was his ultimate comfort zone. But he left it and the other disciples to take a chance by walking on the water to meet Jesus. He starts off just the same as many of us, confident and walking straight ahead. But just like we do, he got distracted by everything that was going on, and started to sink. *"But when he saw the wind boisterous, he was afraid; and beginning to sink, he cried, saying, Lord, save me"* Matthew 14:30.

How many times have we while on our walk with God gotten distracted by things that are going on around us? Peter was doing just fine, walking on the water as long as he kept his eyes on Jesus, but then he started looking around, that was his mistake. The next verse is the most remarkable of all, *"And immediately Jesus stretched forth his hand, and caught him, and said unto him, O thou of little faith, wherefore didst thou doubt?* Matthew 14:31. Jesus was less than an arm's length away from Peter! He did not have to run to Peter to save his life. When Peter called out for Jesus, Jesus was right there in front of him.

Today, step out of your comfort zone. It is not easy. You may actually have to step out in the middle of a storm, leaving behind family, friends or other loved ones, but Jesus is calling you. Do not become so distracted by the things that have kept you comfortable that you fail to realize that Jesus is right there in front of you. He will not let you fail. He will not let you drown. All he is asking is that you "Come".

Day 20: Don't Hold Back

For me, the process of being truly honest about my experiences, the pain, and shame has been a long one. I held the initial secret of the abuse from the first day it happened at age 12, until my parents' divorce at age 23. Even then I only told to ensure that my parents would not reconcile. I never really went into detail about all of the events that happened, or how they made me feel. I felt that just by saying something had happened I had done enough. I went to therapy and only told some of what I felt. I controlled the pain and tears. I didn't even let God in. I told Him I surrendered all, but in reality, I was holding back.

In Acts chapter five, there was a couple named Ananais and Sapphira who owned land that they decided to sell and donate the money to the church. In Acts 5:3 Ananais brought some of the money to the apostle Peter and tried to convince him that it was the full amount. Peter's response was, *"Ananias, why hath Satan filled thine heart to lie to the Holy Ghost, and to keep back part of the price of the land?"* After that, Ananais fell dead right there on the spot. His wife Sapphira was also asked about the price of the land. She also lied about keeping some of the money and fell dead. *"How is it that ye have agreed together to tempt the Spirit of the*

Lord? behold, the feet of them which have buried thy
husband are at the door, and shall carry thee out" Acts 5:9.

God is a merciful God who does not strike us dead for holding
back things from Him, but we cause death to ourselves in
other ways. By allowing the devil to convince us to keep
something back for ourselves, we cannot experience all of
the fullness that God has for us. When we hold on to anger,
we cannot experience God's joy. When we hold onto worry,
we cannot experience His peace. When we hold onto fear,
we cannot experience His perfect love, because the Word
says that *"Perfect love casts out fear"* (I John 4:18).

I believe this story is in the bible to show us the seriousness
of holding back something when we say that we have given it
over to Christ. We must really be honest with ourselves,
because at the end of the day, God knows our hearts. People
may be fooled when we say that we have changed, but God
knows for sure what our intentions are towards Him. If we
say that we are giving everything to Christ, we must. We
cannot hold something back for "just in case".

Ananais and Sapphira had probably convinced themselves
that they needed to keep some of the money from selling
their land in case they fell on hard times. They failed to really
trust God to bless them for their faith in Him. It is hard, I
know. I used to hold on to some anger and worry in case
things did not work out with my marriage and I had to start
again. I held on to some skepticism in case someone I loved

tried to take advantage of me. I held on to some doubt in case really trusting in God meant that I would somehow be hurt. I never really had faith in Him because I didn't believe He had the power to make me new. Once I decided to stop holding back, God was able to get into all of those places in my heart that had turned into stone. For the first time I could experience love, joy, peace, really be patient with people and truly forgive when someone had hurt me.

Today, stop holding back! I know It is a BIG risk. It means giving up something that you think you might need, but it also means gaining something you've never had-the fullness of God's unconditional love.

Day 21: No Turning Back

In our lives as we overcome the many challenges that we face trying to redefine ourselves and a start a new life, there may be times when we think about our previous lives. Sometimes we find ourselves wondering about a person we encountered, or a life we think we may have lost. I know in my journey to become new in Christ, I often took time from a beautiful life with a great career, husband and kids who I adored and returned my affection to think "What if?" I'm sure that I'm not alone in this, but I have discovered God's thoughts about looking back to the good old days.

There is a famous hymn that says "I have decided to follow Jesus, no turning back." Why is that so important? Why does God require that once he delivers us from a situation we do not look back? In Genesis 19 we are able to see the consequences for a person who violated God's rule of not turning back to see again what you have left behind. Lot was Abraham's nephew and lived in a city called Sodom and Gomorrah. This place was described as a VERY sinful city, so much so that God was not even able to find 20 righteous people there to convince him to spare it! Lot and his family were visited there by angels who warned them to leave because God would destroy the city. The inhabitants saw the angels enter Lot's house as men and demanded to have sex with the strangers. *"And they called unto Lot, and said unto him, Where are the men which came in to thee this night?*

bring them out unto us, that we may know them" Genesis 19:5.

God through the angels warned Lot and his family to leave the city. The scripture says that in the morning Lot got his wife and two of his daughters and left the city, Genesis 19: 15. Those were the only possessions that he took with him. Usually, in the bible when someone moves from one place to another, it includes their cattle, servants, and all of their belongings. In this case the move was quick and light.

Lot, his wife and daughters were given strict instructions to move *"Escape for thy life; look not behind thee, neither stay thou in all the plain; escape to the mountain, lest thou be consumed"* Genesis 19:18. As they continued on their journey, Lot's wife looked back at the city that was being destroyed by fire and she ended up being destroyed *"But his wife looked back from behind him, and she became a pillar of salt"* Genesis 19:26. Why did Lot's wife look back? Well, she had daughters and sons-in-law still there who refused to leave at Lot's warning (Genesis 19: 13-14). She had left all of her belongings there, and now would have to start over from scratch. But that was what God wanted. They had lived in a place of extreme sin for so long but God was doing a new thing in them and didn't want any traces of the old life there.

Likewise, God is doing a new thing in all of us. He wants all of our time, energy, and focus on Him. He does not want us looking back at our old lifestyle, friends or even family members as we strive to be perfect in Him. As a mother, Lot's wife may have been influenced by her daughters in sin, and may not have been able to accept everything that God wanted to do in and through her. Her destruction shows us the importance of leaving the sin behind. When God says it's time to move, it's time to go and to travel light. Leave the baggage of the past behind, and allow God to destroy it for good. Do not seek to search through ashes. Go, and go now. Travel light and live. Follow Jesus, no turning back!

New

My hands are still my hands

My feet are still my feet

My heart is still my heart

But it beats a different beat

My arms are still my arms

But they hold with different love

My eyes are still my eyes

But they always look above

My legs are still my legs

Walking in a path each day

That is very unfamiliar

Though I surely know the way

They can't see it yet,

But I don't even care

I still know it's true

And I will always share

I am new inside

God has made me new

Brand new

Inside

Day 22: Forgiveness is For YOU

When I first came to terms with the fact that I had been
sexually abused, I had to do some serious searching not only
of my own soul, but of the heart of God to help me with true
forgiveness. For me, the initial instinct was that I hoped my
father lived a miserable life and died a horrible death for
what he did to me. I wanted him to just drop off of the face
of the earth. He had caused me so much pain throughout
childhood and into adulthood that the thought of existing on
the same planet with him made me physically ill.

Then I came to understand the meaning of true forgiveness
and the impact of it on my own life. I decided that I needed
to forgive my abuser in order to really be able to start again.
It was hard, but necessary. The forgiveness was for me and
my freedom. It did not mean I would accept my father into
my life, have a relationship with him, or allow him within
1,000 feet of my children. It did mean that the place where I
was holding onto the anger and pain toward him would now
be free and open to God for Him to fill with His love and
peace.

Forgiveness is not easy. It is by far the hardest thing I had to
do in my healing process. When someone hurts you in the
way that we've been hurt all our hearts can wish for is
destruction to come upon them. I never thought I could get
to a point where mentioning my abuser's name would not

cause my heart to race. After all, I lived in sheer terror. I could not sleep at night for years because of fear that he was coming into my room. Imagine the countless hours of sleep lost because of his lust. I did not think I could forgive. I lived in a world where I was scared and insecure about myself, my feelings, and my future. Forgiveness seemed so hard. But then I realized that it was not for him, it was for me.

The New Testament is full of scriptures of forgiveness. Colossians 3:13 tells us to *"forgive others as the Lord forgave us"*. Luke 6:37 tells us to *"forgive and be forgiven"*. Matthew 6: 14-16 tells us to *"forgive men so that God will forgive us"*. Mark 11:25 tells us that *"when we pray, if we have a problem with someone to forgive them so that God will forgive us"*. This seems to be a recurring theme. We have to forgive because God forgave us. I had a serious problem with this for many years! I would always say "Well, I'm NOT God. I cannot forgive what has happened to me."

Then I came to understand something. Forgiveness is not about my abuser and me, it is about God and me. By forgiving, I showed God that I have faith in Him to take my pain and turn it into joy. I showed Him that His sacrifice of His only Son was more important to me than my anger. I showed Him that I appreciate what He had done for me, and in turn I will give myself to Him. Forgiveness is the key that unlocks the prison of anger, fear, insecurity, and shame.

Today, ask God to help you forgive your abuser. This does not mean that you have to contact the person and physically say to them "I forgive you." It does not mean you must start a relationship with your abuser as if nothing happened. It also does not mean you must trust this person ever again, or allow them into your life if you do not choose to. However, it does mean that you will agree to free yourself from the prison that has been holding you. It also means that you will allow Christ to fill you with His love. Love so powerful that He gave His life for you. Forgiveness is not for your abuser. Forgiveness is for YOU!!

Day 23: Show Off The New You

Do you ever feel like you have been through so many bad things that you wish you could just disappear? I have had many times in my life where I would wake up and say "I hate my life." Or "I wish I could have another life." It is not easy to face the challenges that are forced upon you when you are abused by someone else. It is hard when the pain that you deal with on a daily basis was caused by actions other that your own. I know I have often felt dirty, embarrassed, or afraid to look at my own reflection in the mirror because of feeling so badly about myself.

Knowing that, it's easy to relate to the ten lepers Jesus encountered in Luke 17. Lepers in ancient society were physically outcast and quarantined from the rest of the city inhabitants because of the severity of their disease. The leprosy caused such infectious boils that could not be cured, that people who somehow contracted this condition was immediately ostracized from their friends, family, and other members of the city. They were seen as cursed because the condition had no known cause.

In Luke 17 we see Jesus teaching in parables about forgiveness, faith, and servitude when he encountered the ten lepers. These men did not ask much of Jesus, simply for him to have mercy on them. *And as he entered into a certain village, there met him ten men that were lepers, which stood afar off: And they lifted up their voices, and said, Jesus, Master, have mercy on us"* Luke 17: 12-13.

Jesus saw the lepers, those who had been outcast by their society and healed them. But not only that, he gave them specific instructions to go and show themselves to the priests. Why the priests? Why not their spouses, children, parents or other loved ones? During these times, the priests were the ones within tribes, villages or cities who would determine the diagnosis of leprosy. An individual who was presumed to have these symptoms would have to present him or herself to the priest. If the diagnosis was unclear, the person would be quarantined for seven days. Once more symptoms presented, the person would be kicked outside of the city and declared unclean.

Has someone made a negative declaration over your life? Has someone declared you unclean because of what they can see on the outside? Today, like the ten lepers, call out to Jesus to have mercy on you. Like the lepers, he will cleanse you, but it will require some action on your part. *"And when he saw them, he said unto them, Go shew yourselves unto the priests. And it came to pass, that, as they went, they were cleansed."* Luke 17:14. **As they went, they were cleaned**. In order for them to be cured of their disease they had to be prepared to face those who had looked down upon them and publicly cast them out.

We also must not be ashamed to look those people in the face who have turned their backs on us. They may have publicly embarrassed us or humiliated us because something that was not our fault. We may have been disgraced because of what has become of our bodies. But today, Jesus wants us to know that he does have mercy on us. We should not be ashamed of what has happened. We should go, in faith, following God's word knowing that His grace is sufficient for us. As we walk in His Word, we too will be healed. Be ready to show off your new self!!

Day 24: Giving Your Best to Christ

During this time of renewal in your mind, body, and spirit you will probably meet people who just don't get why you're doing what you're doing. Sometimes I have met people who wonder why I pray as much, as long, or as hard as I do now. They wonder why I am as nice as I am even to people who I used to tell off. What they don't understand is that God is doing a work inside of me that can be seen on the outside to others who are really watching. This is the same for all of us who have overcome the abuse.

What happened when we were abused happened behind closed doors and in secret. The result was a different person who others may have noticed a change in, but not really known why. Likewise, when we let God enter into those secret places of our hearts where we have been hurt, He heals and touches us behind closed doors. The result is a change that people can observe outwardly though they may not necessarily understand why it has happened.

This same kind of story can be observed in Matthew 26:7, when Jesus was eating at the house of Simon, a few days before his crucifixion. A woman came into where he was carrying an alabaster box with very expensive oil inside; *"There came unto him a woman having an alabaster box of very precious ointment, and poured it on his head, as he sat at meat."* To us, this may not seem like such a big deal, but to those watching the scene, this was incredible. Alabaster was a very expensive material that was a symbol of purity, and was only used for special occasions. Also, the oil inside was costly, and in this instance was just poured on Jesus' head. The disciples sitting with Jesus at the meal were outraged that this woman had essentially just wasted her best on Jesus. They suggested that she should have kept this oil to sell, and give the money to the poor, *"But when his disciples saw it, they had indignation, saying, To what purpose is this waste? For this ointment might have been sold for much, and given to the poor"* Matthew 26: 8-9. Jesus reprimanded the disciples, letting them know that this woman had done a good thing.

According to various bible scholars this woman was a prostitute who poured her most expensive oil on Jesus, and washed his feet with her hair. There is so much symbolism in that text. She was using her alabaster box, a sign of purity, containing expensive oil, to give to Jesus and then washing his feet with her crowning glory-her hair. In essence, she gave all of her best to Jesus, and in return, he accepted her gifts. He did not cast her out, ridicule her or reprimand her like the disciples did. As a matter of fact, he HONORED her! *"Verily I say unto you, Wheresoever this gospel shall be preached in the whole world, there shall also this, that this woman hath done, be told for a memorial of her."* Matthew 26:13.

Today, commit to giving your best to Christ. Don't be afraid of what others will think. God is doing a work in all of us, that only we can understand. Jesus appreciates our outward sacrifice to Him as thanks for all that He is doing on the inside. And just like the woman with the alabaster box, because of the good work that you will do for Christ, there will be a memorial of YOU for giving God your best.

Day 25: Willing to Do Whatever It Takes

As a kid growing up, I watched my brothers play a game called "ghost driver". They would ride their bikes up to the top of the hill in front of our house, turn around, and start back downhill. Halfway through the hill they would jump off of their bikes and see how far the bikes would go with a "ghost driver". My brothers were risk takers. They did not mind falling down, being hurt-sometimes badly, or even destroying their property. They enjoyed the thrill of what happened when you risk it all.

There was a lady in Mark who was a risk taker. She is known as the woman with the issue of blood. The scripture says that she had suffered with this condition for 12 years and had spent all the money that she had going to doctors, who only made her worse. *"And a certain woman, which had an issue of blood twelve years, And had suffered many things of many physicians, and had spent all that she had, and was nothing bettered, but rather grew worse"* Mark 5:25-26. This was going on with the woman for 12 years, when she reached a point where she decided enough was enough and she was willing to risk everything, even her life for her healing.

In the text, the story continues with Jesus being pressed by a crowd of people. This woman says within herself that if she can just touch the hem of Jesus' garment, she will be made well. The "hem" of Jesus' garment meant she was willing to get down on the ground and crawl through the crowd to get to Him. She did not aim for the collar or the sleeve, but the hem. She was willing to do whatever it took! She was a risk taker because in those days, a woman who was unclean was not allowed to associate with others in her community, and doing so would result in a punishment of being stoned. This lady reached such a point of desperation that she was willing to risk even her life to be free of the condition that had held her captive for over a decade. The bible tells us that when she touched Jesus' clothes He actually felt some power go from Him. He asked who had touched Him, and she confessed. Then he said to her, *"Daughter, thy faith hath made thee whole; go in peace, and be whole of thy plague"* Mark 5:34.

Why did Jesus tell this lady that her faith had made her whole? After all, He had the power to heal. She touched Him and was instantly healed. What did her faith have to do with it? It was her faith that convinced her that enough was enough, and that she had to find Jesus. It was her faith that caused her to risk being stoned by her community to go out into the crowd where Jesus was. It was her faith that led her to believe in Jesus so strongly that she did not mind crawling on the ground for her healing. It was her faith that caused her to come forth and admit to Jesus that she had touched Him. Her faith in Jesus was so strong that out of all of the people in the crowd, He noticed her and healed her.

Where is your faith in God? Are you willing to do whatever it takes to get to Jesus? Are you willing to risk everything-including your life to get close enough to Him to truly be healed? Surely you, like this woman have sought many things in life to make you feel better, only to leave you feeling worse. Now it's time to press toward Jesus. Press past traditions, rules, and ideas about who is holy and who is not. Today is your day, now is the time. Be willing to do whatever it takes to get close enough to Jesus to be healed. Have faith in His power, knowing that like this woman your faith will make you whole.

Day 26: You Gotta Fight For Your Right (to be blessed)

There would be days when I would be so depressed the sight of my reflection in the mirror would cause me to sob. I was so devastated by what had happened to me and what I had done as a result of my own pain that I couldn't even stand to look at myself. I would always wish bad things for myself like sickness. I had a hard time accepting compliments from friends, loved ones, co-workers, or even perfect strangers. It was like I felt like I didn't deserve anything good. Then one day God's Word took control of my mind, and I started to understand how He viewed me. From there my perspective about myself changed. I decided that I deserved the best out of life and nothing less than the best would do.

This is sort of like what Jacob (Genesis) experienced. Jacob was the younger son of Isaac and grandson of Abraham. Yet, he was a shady character. Jacob made his older twin brother Esau trade his birthright for a pot of stew. As if that wasn't good enough, Jacob then tricked their father Isaac into giving him Esau's inheritance while Isaac was on his death bed! Jacob had lived a life of trickery. He had betrayed people who loved him, and in exchange, he had been betrayed when he tried to get married. He was living a life where he constantly had to look over his shoulder because he had started so much drama with his family.

Finally, in Genesis 32 we see that Jacob has reached a place in his life where he wants to reunite with his brother. He gets his family and servants together to travel to be with Esau. I can imagine that he felt a little nervous about approaching a brother he had deceived twice. In the text, Genesis 32: 22-23, we see that Jacob sent everyone in his party ahead to continue the journey and he stayed behind, alone. While Jacob was alone, an angel appeared to him and he wrestled with the angel all night long-so much that his thigh was out of joint. The angel commanded that Jacob let him go, but Jacob refused *"And he said, Let me go, for the day breaketh. And he said, I will not let thee go, except thou bless me."* Genesis 32:26. Jacob was physically hurt from his trial, but in the end he refused to give up until he got his blessing, and the bible says that *"he blessed him there. And Jacob called the name of the place Peniel: for I have seen God face to face, and my life is preserved"* Genesis 32: 29b-30

Today, we have to challenge ourselves to get to the place where Jacob was. We have all been through terrible things. Some have been perpetrated against us, and some, if we're honest with ourselves, we have perpetrated. But to God that doesn't matter. It didn't matter to Him that Jacob was sneaky and a professional con-man. It didn't matter that Jacob had tricked his own brother and father. What is important to realize however, is that when Jacob made up his mind that he was ready to turn his life around, he had to fight for his blessing. He had to send his family away. He had to get by himself so that he could have a personal encounter with God. For him, it required a physical struggle.

This may be the case for you as well. You may have to give up drinking alcohol, or using drugs. Maybe food consumption is your battle. Whatever it is that is holding you back, you have to be willing to send it away. Like Jacob, you may end your spiritual battle with a physical mark of some sort. There may be weight loss or gain, hair loss or gain. For me, there is a grey patch of hair above my right temple. But every time I look in the mirror now, instead of crying from my reflection, I praise God; because like Jacob I know that "I have seen God face to face, and my life is preserved."

Day 27:No More Excuses

On the night I was molested, I decided that I could not trust my father. I wasn't sure what I could do or who I could trust, but I knew that my home was no longer a safe place for me. The next morning I made a decision to be the best student possible so that I would be able to go to any college of my choosing without having to worry about admission. As time went on and my home life got worse I decided that I had to not only go to college, but I had to go as far away from my home as possible to really be free. Not trusting people who are supposed to love you was a part of my being. It was a part of my daily interaction with people. There was never a time where I had really and fully trusted another person. I didn't know how, and honestly I wasn't sure I could. It was easier to explain why I was the way I was than to change, but I knew I had to. I was paralyzed by my inability to trust.

In John chapter five there is a paralyzed man that has been sitting by a pool for 38 years. There was a group of sick people waiting for an angel to come once a year to stir up the water. Whoever could make it into the pool after that would be healed. When Jesus saw the man lying there he asked a simple question, *"Do you want to get well?"* John 5:6 (NIV). Jesus was asking the man if he wanted to be healed. Instead of saying to Jesus, "Yes Lord! I have been like this for 38 years. I'd love the chance to walk again!" he replied with excuses; *"Sir, I have no one to help me into the pool when the water is stirred. While I am trying to get in, someone else goes down ahead of me"* John 5:7 (NIV). Jesus didn't give the man a chance to come up with any more reasons why he couldn't change. He just replied, *"Get up! Pick up your mat and walk"* John 5:8.

The paralyzed man was telling Jesus that he had tried to get better before, but someone else was in the way. I was like that man for many years. I was telling Jesus about all of the people who were in my way and stopping my ability to change. I would say things like "Well, if my father hadn't done this to me, I would be able to trust." Or "If someone was able to pick up on the signs (like me refusing to eat for weeks at a time as a teenager), I would be able to be more understanding to others." But at the end of the day none of that mattered. Standing in front of my face was Jesus challenging me to pick up my mat of excuses and walk in the destiny that He had called me to.

Today, Jesus is asking you if you want to get well. He already knows all about your situation. He knows why you are where you are in life. To Him, none of that matters or affects His ability to make you whole again. The text says that *"At once the man was cured; he picked up his mat and walked"* John 5:9. The man was cured instantly and walked. The scripture does not say he hopped, limped, or needed support walking. It says he "walked". Jesus wants to get us back on our own two feet and walking stably in Him. He has a plan for all of our lives, but first we have to stop making excuses.

He already knows everything about you. He knows about everyone who has been a part of getting you to the bad place where you've been. Today He is standing right in front of you and wants to know, "Do YOU want to get well?" Stop lying on your mat of excuses and allow Him to show you how to walk. It's up to you now!

Day 28: Friends versus "Friends"

Being a victim of sexual abuse is isolating. It happens to you all alone, and leaves you feeling alone. For me it was hard to make true friends because I wasn't sure who I could trust with my secret. At home in childhood I was VERY quiet and reserved. At school I was very outgoing and popular everyone "knew" me, but yet nobody really knew me. At the height of my attempts to further hide my true feelings of shame and insecurity, I got on a social networking website. I added anyone and everyone who asked me to be a "friend" because I liked that feeling of once again being popular. I posted pictures of myself and my family and constantly updated my actions and whereabouts because it felt good to have so many "friends". Yet, when I was really at my lowest point, of the 541 people I called "friends" there were only three I could really talk to.

Ruth and Naomi were true friends. Ruth was a poor widow from a foreign land who befriended and took care of her older mother-in-law, Naomi. They traveled together to Bethlehem in time for a harvest, where Naomi introduced Ruth to her relative Boaz. Boaz was fond of Ruth and allowed her to work in his fields, taking the leftover grain from the harvest because he had heard what a wonderful daughter-in-law she had been to Naomi. Ruth continued to work faithfully in the fields gathering grain, and always remembered to take her goods to Naomi every night. One day Boaz became so impressed with her, that he took Ruth as his wife. After all of her struggle and hard times, she had gone from poor widow to rich wife, who was also able to have a son. Naomi came to live with Ruth and Boaz, and to help care for their baby son Obed. (Ruth chapters 1-4 all)

 When Ruth made that major transition, she did not forget about Naomi who had stood by her when she was down and out. She did not forget that Naomi had taken her when she moved back to Bethlehem. Ruth remembered that it was her mother-in-law who introduced her to Boaz in the first place so that she could have a fresh start. Just as Naomi had been a true friend to Ruth, Ruth was a true friend to Naomi.

Do you have true friends? Do you have people who will stand by you during bad times and help you get to the good? Will your friends try to keep you down or help you get back on your own two feet? Proverbs 17:17 says that "A friend loves at _all_ times". Naomi could have left Ruth behind and moved on to her homeland to live with Boaz by herself, but she did not. She realized that Ruth needed her, and in turn Ruth repaid her kindness. This was a true friendship, give and take. Neither put themselves above the other, but both were looking out for one another.

Today, take inventory of the people in your life that you call "friends". Are they looking out for you? Are you looking out for them? Is the relationship based on give and take, or all take? When you get to a place where you are stronger and have fully regained confidence in who you are in God, will they be happy for you, or hate on you? The bible says in Proverbs 18:24 that, *"The man of many friends [a friend of all the world] will prove himself a bad friend, but there is a friend who sticks closer than a brother."* Ask God to show you this friend in your life, and in turn ask Him to enable you to be this friend for someone else.

Day 29: You Gotta Give Something to Get Something

Have you ever had someone look you square in your eyes and ask "Why are you so angry?" For me, that those were fighting words! People who have not been abused cannot understand how hard it is to wake up every day with sadness and depression in your heart. They have little compassion for the fact that while everyone around you lives and enjoys life, you are angry. Angry because your life has been stolen. Angry because no one is doing anything about it. Angry because you don't know what to do about it. Angry because you cannot verbalize how you feel and no one can read your mind. Angry because in a room full of people you feel completely alone. Why are you so angry? How could you not be? I held on to my anger for dear life. It was my calling card. Anyone and everyone knew not to mess with me, because I would definitely take your head off and hand it to you if you crossed me.

Zacchaeus had the same kind of reputation. In Luke 19, there is a very short story about a tax collector. He was a hated man, because tax collectors worked for foreign oppressors (Romans) who exploited the Jews. Since the Romans wanted to be as efficient as possible they would hire other Jews to collect taxes in their local areas. It was like Zacchaeus was a traitor! The more money he collected from his own people, the bigger commission he got from the Romans. He had NO friends because no one could trust his intentions!

When Jesus came to the town where Zacchaeus was, a crowd followed. Zacchaeus was so short that climbed into a tree to see Jesus. Immediately Jesus saw Zacchaeus and called him down from the tree. He announced that he would go to Zacchaeus' house. *"Zacchaeus, come down immediately. I must stay at your house today"* Luke 19:5. People in the crowd got upset about Jesus' choice and said *"He has gone to be the guest of a sinner..."* (Luke 19: 7), but Jesus knew Zacchaeus' heart. Right away Zacchaeus repented for taking so much from the people and promised to refund everyone their money plus four times what he had taken. *"Zacchaeus stood up and said to the Lord, "Look, Lord! Here and now I give half of my possessions to the poor, and if I have cheated anybody out of anything, I will pay back four times the amount"* Luke 19:8. Zacchaeus knew that getting Jesus to stay with him was more important than what he had been holding onto.

What do you have? I know in my anger I took peace and joy from my family. My anger probably embezzled some sanity from my husband. I extorted some trust from friends. When I really saw Jesus and realized that he saw me too, I wanted to change. Zacchaues' giving all of that money away no doubt meant he would be fired. His whole identity would have to change because he was no longer a tax collector. He would have to deal with just being a regular short guy, not a tough

95

tax collector. Even still, he chose to give it all up for a chance to really get to know Jesus.

Today, are you willing to give up what you've had for Him? Only He can replace your anger with joy, your worry with peace and your insecurity with an understanding of who you are in Him. He sees you. He sees all of us. Maybe we go up into trees to be above everyone else, or below the crowd to be beneath, but He is still there. He sees you. He wants to go home with YOU. He doesn't care what you've done or who you've hurt, He has still chosen you. The question is; are you willing to give up what you have been holding on to for Him?

HE Wants ME

He wants me

He loves me

When no one else can see

How hard I am trying

To be all I can be

He needs me

He shows me

How to do things His way

So I can start anew

Starting with today

He likes me

He knows that

I will be just fine

Cuz He gave me His life

And He has taken mine

Day 30: He Will Shut the Haters Up

Sometimes there are days when God speaks something into my spirit that just seems impossible. Like when he told me to write these devotionals. It seemed ridiculous! I am a psychometrician by trade, not a psychologist or psychiatrist. I was an abuse victim, who was still dealing with my own fears and insecurity. I was not rich, in fact I had no idea how to get a book published. But somehow God had chosen me anyway. It was not optional. I had decided to yield my will to His, and He used me in the way that was best. I couldn't tell everyone about the book, because some would think it was outrageous. I just had to be quiet and let God do His work in and through me.

This is what Zacharias and Elisabeth faced in Luke 1: 7. They had prayed for many years for a child but she was unable to have one, and the couple had grown into old age. One day an angel of the Lord came to Zacharias and told them that God had heard his prayers and that Elisabeth would have a baby. Zacharias was overwhelmed! This was something they had prayed for and finally the prayer was answered. On the other hand, he thought about the reality that they were both very old, and having a baby seemed next to impossible. For his unbelief, Zacharias was made unable to speak. *"And, behold, thou shalt be dumb, and not able to speak, until the day that these things shall be performed, because thou believest not my words, which shall be fulfilled in their season"* Luke 1:13.

Sometimes God will put you in a place where people around you cannot verbalize their unbelief. Zacharias had been praying for this miracle for so many years that he thought his problem was bigger than God's power. The angel said that Zacharias was not able to speak "until the day that these things shall be performed." He had to keep quiet until God had completed His work. God was creating a new life inside of Elisabeth. Imagine the stress and strain of pregnancy and childbirth along with her own spouse saying that she was too old in the first place. God had to shut Zacharias' mouth so that Elisabeth could focus on the miracle growing inside of her.

How many times during your new walk with God have you tried to share what He's doing in your life? Sometimes you're met with support, sometimes you're met with doubt and "Girl, I don't know about that." When God is doing a new thing inside of us, He only needs us to surrender our will to His. He does not need our permission, or better yet the validation of our friends and family. Regardless of what Zacharias thought about his old wife having a new baby, God was going to do it, so he prevented Zacharias' ability to share his doubts with anyone.

Just like Zacharias, God will close the mouths of those around you who doubt what He's doing in your life. God is giving you a new life. Like a fetus, it starts off small, and no one around you can see it, but you feel it move inside of you and you know it's real. You need to take time to make sure the new life is developing properly so that when it is presented to the world there will be no defects.

Today, only focus on that new life inside of you. Focus on the newness in its infancy. Don't worry about those around you and their opinions about you starting over at this point. God will shut them up for their unbelief and will only allow them to speak on the day that He has performed His work in you!

Day 31: You CAN Make a Difference

When God told me to write this book for survivors of sexual abuse, I fought my own thoughts many times. I am not a therapist, or counselor. In fact, I was in therapy and counseling myself. My marriage was barely holding on because of years of my acting out as a result of my own pain. I was taking medicine for depression and suicidal ideation, yet God chose me to reach out to others who were in pain. I in no way felt qualified to write such a book, but somehow I was able to see past my own human flaws, and submit myself as an open vessel to be used by God for His purposes.

It seems that even in Jesus' time there were people who questioned whether or not they were truly qualified to help someone else. In Luke 10: 30 Jesus tells a story about a man who was on a journey and met a group of thieves who beat him, robbed him, and left him on the side of the road. While this man was lying by the side of the road, a priest passed by him and did nothing. Next a Levite (a descendant of Moses) passed him by without helping. Finally, a Samaritan saw the man on the ground and helped him, *"But a certain Samaritan, as he journeyed, came where he was: and when he saw him, he had compassion on him, And went to him, and bound up his wounds, pouring in oil and wine, and set him on his own beast, and brought him to an inn, and took care of him"* Luke 10: 33-34. You may have heard the story of the "Good Samaritan" many times and not understood the significance in it. A Samaritan was considered a "dog" in those times, because it was a person who was half Jew, half pagan. Samaritans were not included in mainstream Jewish society because their blood was not pure.

Somehow, this person who was not technically qualified to help anyone, and was looked down upon, was used by God to help someone in need. The priest who was definitely qualified did not help. The Levite from a royal Jewish bloodline also missed an opportunity to reach out. Only the Samaritan knew what it was like to be ignored by people who had the power to help. Because of this, the bible says that he had compassion on the man and bandaged him up, gave him something to drink, and took care of him. The act of kindness shown by this man lets us know that we do not have to be in high positions of power or from royalty to help someone else.

God allowed me to write these devotionals for you because I know what you feel. Like the Samaritan man, I know what it's like to be ashamed of something that is not your fault. I know the pain that you feel in being left to deal with hurt caused by someone who was supposed to protect you. And like the Samaritan, I allowed God to use me to reach out to you-hurting, left by the side of the road because you have been robbed and stripped by your past.

In the same way, God wants to use you too. You have a special story and experience that others can relate to. The experience of an over comer of sexual abuse is one that is unique. Many people say "I understand", but few actually do. Today, allow God to use your past to help another who may not otherwise get help. Do you know someone who is really struggling in life? Maybe you have thought about that person many times, and think to yourself that you are not qualified. Well, you are. You have made it through your circumstances so that you can be aware of a person who is down. Do not get so caught up in your journey that you fail to look down and see what's beneath you. Someone is still down. Someone is being passed by. Let God's compassion allow you to be a <u>Good Samaritan</u> today.

You are Called for Such a Time as This

If you have reached this page of the book you have hopefully read all 31 days of devotionals. You have prayed for at least 31 days in a row, and have read 31 passages of scripture. You may have read more than what was recommended each day- which is great! You may have uncovered some new things about God, yourself, and your daily interactions with others. You may also have had some memories of your abuser, and discovered some new strategies for how to deal with that person. It is my sincere prayer that you have gained a renewed faith in God, in His ability to restore you, and your ability to be restored. This final portion of the book is not a closing however, it is a call to action for a new beginning.

Now that you have essentially opened yourself up to God, His call for your life, and His will for you, you might wonder what to do with this new knowledge. How can you take what you have learned to be a blessing to others?

As with every other devotional, of course there is a biblical story that answers this question for you. In the book of Esther, we discover a young girl who comes from a people who had been exiled. She was adopted by her uncle Mordecai and lived in a new land. The King of the land became enraged with his wife and banished her as Queen. He summoned a group of virgins to his palace for inspection and a 12 month beautification process. Once Esther completed the process, she was chosen as the new Queen. She went from a place of banishment to a place of royalty!

Because of the treatment of the Jews, Queen Esther did not reveal to anyone that she was a Jew. One day there was a plot to kill all of the Jews in the land. Esther's uncle Mordecai was very saddened by this and stood outside of the king's gate weeping and wearing ashcloth, which was the cloth of mourning. Esther tried to get him to stop, but he would not. In fact, when he finally had the chance to speak with her, Mordecai said to his niece, *"who knoweth whether thou art come to the kingdom for such a time as this?"* Esther 4:14. Esther knew she had a responsibility to her people, and revealed to the king that she was a Jew. This revelation caused an entire race of people to be saved.

The same can be applied to you. You have first been able to admit that you were abused. By reading this book, you were willing to take the time to study God's Word as it relates to various topics surrounding the abuse, and the feelings that stemmed from it. You were able to get to the end, and prayerfully are feeling more encouraged and confident as it relates to your healing. Perhaps you have even sought out a health care professional who can help you work through the feelings and emotions as they arise. Hopefully you have also found a supportive group of people, either family or friends who you can trust to be vulnerable with as you continue on your road to healing.

All of these things are wonderful! They will help you make a transition from banishment to royalty, but what about that person who is still outside of the king's gate? There are others who have been abused. According to the National Center for the Prevention and Treatment of Child Abuse, over 68% of children who are sexually abused, are abused by a family member. Thirty one percent of women, and fourteen percent of men in prison in the United States were sexually abused as children. A total of 7.6% of the children in the

United States report cases of sexual abuse every year-and there are many cases that go unreported due to issues such as fear of the abuser. This fight is NOT over!! There are still people out there who are hurting. They come in all races, ages, genders and socioeconomic backgrounds. They are at the king's gate, weeping, and wearing ashcloth. Will you ignore them, or help them to come in, hear what they have to say, and find a way to help?

I will admit I am blessed. Though I was abused, I have a great family who believed me. I have a great job and medical benefits so that I could get the mental help I needed through counseling and medication. I have an amazing spouse who supports me every step of the way through my healing process. I have a strong network of friends and close spiritual leadership to keep me encouraged and my faith strong. But I know that everyone is not as fortunate.

The ability to reach others who have been abused it one that is unique to us, the survivors. We really know what the pain feels like, how it runs through your veins as real as your own blood. We know what it means to want to kill yourself just because you know of no other way to escape your own body. We know, we understand, and we are charged with a mission to reach others whose story is similar to ours.

Today, as you conclude this book, I admonish you to reach out to those still outside of the king's gate. There are many, I'm sure. You may not feel prepared, educated or adequate, but you have been called. And just like Mordecai said to Esther, who knows whether YOU have come into the kingdom for such a time as this?

Pass this book and the scripture messages within on to another to encourage them. Revelations 12:11 says *"And they overcame him by the blood of the Lamb, and by the word of their testimony."* **Remember, you are blessed to be a blessing!!**

7400944R0

Made in the USA
Charleston, SC
27 February 2011